A Prayer a Day

From Advent to Epiphany

David Adam

Augsburg Books

MINNEAPOLIS

A PRAYER A DAY FROM ADVENT TO EPIPHANY

The publishers wish to express their gratitude to the
copyright holders who have granted permission to include
their material in this book. Every effort has been made to
trace the copyright holders of all the songs in this collection
and we hope that no copyright has been infringed. Apology
is made and pardon sought if the contrary be the case, and
a correction will be made in any reprint of this book.

Collects from Common Worship: Services and Prayers for
the Church of England are copyright © The Archbishops
Council 2000. Material from this work is reproduced with
permission.

Cover image: Cover art by Gama5 from iStock
Cover design: Alisha Lofgren

Print ISBN: 978-1-5064-5904-2

Contents

Foreword   5

First Sunday of Advent   7

Days 2–20   8

December 17–23   19

Christmas Eve   26

Christmas Day   26

December 26–January 5   27

Epiphany   32

Foreword

Advent has become one of the neglected seasons of the Church year. Its memory is kept on in Advent calendars that count down the days to Christmas, but although there has been a return to lighting Advent candles, in many churches this is often done with few words and little ceremony. It is important that we capture again the expectation and waiting of this season. We must not let Advent be squeezed out by the rush and commercial pressures of modern Christmas festivities. Advent is a very special time. It offers us light in the darkest of days; it opens us up in heart and mind for the coming of our Lord; and it celebrates the God who is always with us and comes to us every moment of our lives. To keep Advent is to prepare properly not only for Christmas but for the God who comes to us.

Advent happens at the darkest time of the year, and it is the shortest day of the year, but it is looking forward to the coming of the light, the coming of Christ to the world. When Christ comes, the days lengthen and the light strengthens. Christmas is about our being delivered from darkness and the shadow of death. Today many people live in the dark because they have not learned to celebrate that the light has come—God comes to us. I often affirm, "When the days are dark and cold, our God comes as he did to our ancestors of old."

By tradition, Advent celebrates three comings of God: God came to the patriarchs and prophets, the people of the past; God came in Jesus Christ for us and for our salvation; God will come again to judge the living and the dead.

But Advent also asks us to realize that God comes to us now. God is with us. God comes to us in love. I take to heart the words of Angelus Silesius (1624–1677):

Though Christ a thousand times
in Bethlehem be born,
if he is not born in you,
you are still forlorn.

And I pray regularly:

O come to my heart, Lord Jesus,
there is room in my heart for thee.

Emily Elizabeth Steele Elliott (1836–1897)

There is a danger of Advent prayers suggesting we have control over God! I often pray, "Lord, come down, come in, come among us." In doing so, am I making God come? Am I causing God to act? Of course not; our God is always coming to us, always with us. But we often ignore God and fail to acknowledge his presence in our lives. Advent is a time of opening ourselves to the God who comes; it is a time of deepening our awareness that God comes to us, is with us.

Make Advent a time when you truly let God into your heart and your home. Make sure your faith is at home in your home, and that you are at home with your faith. There are still too many people who look upon prayer as a long-distance call when in reality God is present and waiting to meet us. Our God comes today and comes to us—to you. Advent celebrates this joy. May the prayers in this book help you to celebrate the God who is, who is with you, and who comes to you.

David Adam

First Sunday of Advent

Almighty God,
give us grace to cast away the works of darkness
and put on the armor of light,
now in the time of this mortal life,
in which your Son Jesus Christ
came to us in great humility;
that on the last day
when he shall come again in his glorious majesty
to judge the living and the dead,
we may rise to the life immortal;
through him who is alive and reigns with you,
in the unity of the Holy Spirit,
one God, now and forever.

Collect for the First Sunday of Advent
Common Worship

Day 2

Our Lord, come!

1 Corinthians 16:22

Amen. Come, Lord Jesus!

Revelation 22:20

I wait for the Lord: my soul waits;
and in his word I hope;
my soul waits for the Lord,
more than those who watch for the morning.

Psalm 130:5, 6

Day 3

Stir up your power, O Lord,
and with great might come among us;
and because we are sorely let
and hindered by our sins,
let your bountiful grace and mercy
speedily help and deliver us;
through Jesus Christ our Lord.

Gelasian Sacramentary (Eighth Century)

Day 4

O God of all hope and joy,
open our hearts in welcome,
that your Son Jesus Christ at his coming
may find in us a dwelling prepared for himself;
who lives and reigns with you and the Holy Spirit,
one God now and forever.

A New Zealand Prayer Book:
He Karakia Mihinare o Aotearoa (1989)

Day 5

Come, O Lord,
open our eyes to your presence,
open our minds to your grace,
open our lips to your praises,
open our hearts to your love,
open our lives to your healing,
and be known among us.

Day 6

Lord God, awaken me
to the beauty of the world
and to the wonders of creation.
Awaken me to your love
and to your coming to me this day.
As you came to the patriarchs and prophets,
you come to me:
help me to be aware of your coming.

Day 7

Hear Jesus say,
"I stand at the door and knock;
at the door of your home,
at the door of your heart,
I come to you.
Open your life to me."

Come, Lord Jesus.

Day 8

Song

Christ is coming. Christ is coming.
Do you know? Do you know?
Are you ready for him?
Are you ready for him?
Yes, I am. Yes, I am.
Are you ready for him?
Are you ready for him?
Yes, I am. Yes, I am.

Tune: "I Hear Thunder"

Day 9

Lord, awaken me to your love.
Make me aware that you come to me
today and every day.
Help me to rejoice in your coming
and in your abiding presence.

Day 10

Blessed are you, Lord my God,
for you sent messengers and prophets
to tell of your coming.
You sent John the Baptist
to help us to prepare your way.
Help me to show your presence
in my daily life and in my work.

Day 11

Song

Jesus, come among us
with your glorious light.
Jesus, come among us;
help us do what's right.

Jesus, come among us;
come now and every day.
Jesus, come among us,
hear us as we pray.

Tune: Caswall ("Glory Be to Jesus")

Day 12

O Lord, you have set before us the great hope
that your kingdom shall come on earth,
and have taught us to pray for its coming:
give us grace to discern
the signs of its dawning,
and to work for the perfect day
when your will shall be done on earth
as it is in heaven;
through Jesus Christ our Lord.

The Promise of His Glory (1991)

Day 13

Come, O Christ my Light,
and illumine my darkness.
Come, my Life,
and revive me from death.
Come, my Physician,
and heal my wounds.
Come, Flame of Divine Love,
and burn up the thorns of my sins,
kindling my heart with the flame of your love.
For you alone are my King and my Lord.

St. Dimitri of Rostov (Seventeenth Century)

Day 14

Come, true light.
Come, life eternal.
Come, hidden mystery.
Come, treasure without name.
Come, reality beyond all words.
Come, person beyond all understanding.
Come, rejoicing without end.
Come, light that knows no evening.
Come, unfailing expectation of the saved.
Come, raising of the fallen.
Come, resurrection of the dead.

St. Symeon the New Theologian (949–1022)

Day 15

Come, all-powerful,
for unceasingly you create, refashion, and change
all things by your will alone.
Come, invisible whom none may touch or handle.
Come, for you continue always unmoved,
yet at every instant you are wholly in movement;
you draw near to us who lie in hell,
yet you remain higher than the heavens.
Come, for your name fills our hearts
with longing and is ever on our lips;
yet who you are and what your nature is,
we cannot say or know.
Come, Alone to the alone.
Come, for you are yourself the desire that is within me.
Come, my breath and my life.
Come, the consolation of my humble soul.
Come, my joy, my glory, my endless delight.

St. Symeon the New Theologian (949–1022)

Day 16

Come, Lord Jesus, draw near; come, Lord:
come among us.
Come as our Savior; come, Lord:
come among us.
Come as our Friend; come, Lord:
come among us.
Come as the Light; come, Lord:
come among us.
Come and we shall be saved; come, Lord:
come among us.

Day 17

O Lord our God,
make us watchful, keep us faithful
as we wait for the coming of your Son our Lord;
that when he shall appear,
he may find us not sleeping in sin,
but active in his service and joyful in his praise;
for the glory of your holy name.

Gelasian Sacramentary (Eighth Century)

Day 18

Come, Lord Jesus, Light of the World,
conquer the darkness
about me and within me.
Come, Lord Jesus.

Come, Lord Jesus, Giver of Life,
conquering death,
restore me and refresh me.
Come, Lord Jesus.

Day 19

Keep us, O Lord,
while we tarry on this earth,
in a serious seeking after you
and in an affectionate walking with you,
every day of our lives;
that when you come,
we may be found not hiding our talent,
nor serving the flesh,
nor yet asleep with our lamp unfurnished,
but waiting and longing for our Lord,
our glorious God forever.

Richard Baxter (1615–1691)

Day 20

When I close my eyes in prayer,
come, Lord Jesus.
When I cry out in the dark,
come, Lord Jesus.
When I struggle with life,
come, Lord Jesus.
When I feel lost or alone,
come, Lord Jesus.
In my celebrations and joy,
come, Lord Jesus.
In my sharing with friends,
come, Lord Jesus.
In my seeking to work for you,
come, Lord Jesus.
When I call upon your name,
come, Lord Jesus.

December 17

O Sapientia

Come with your grace and goodness;
come to my heart and change me.
Come, wisdom of God.
Come, Christ my Lord.

Come with your peace and power;
come to my life and strengthen me.
Come, wisdom of God.
Come, Christ my Lord.

Come with your light and love;
come to my darkness and enlighten me.
Come, wisdom of God.
Come, Christ my Lord.

December 18

O Adonai

Lord of the living water,
quench my thirst and refresh me.
Maranatha.
Come, Lord Jesus.

Lord of the Bread of Heaven,
fill me and strengthen me.
Maranatha.
Come, Lord Jesus.

Lord, my Friend and Savior,
redeem me and bring me to the Promised Land.
Maranatha.
Come, Lord Jesus.

December 19

O Radix Jesse

Jesus, Word made flesh.
Maranatha.
Come, Lord, dwell among us.

Jesus, born of the house of David.
Maranatha.
Come, Lord, dwell among us.

Jesus, born of the blessed Virgin Mary.
Maranatha.
Come, Lord, dwell among us.

Jesus, from the realm of glory.
Maranatha.
Come, Lord, dwell among us.

December 20

O Clavis David

O Key of David,
you open to us your love.
Come, Lord,
be known among us.

O Key of David,
you come to set the prisoner free.
Come, Lord,
be known among us.

O Key of David,
you open to us the kingdom of heaven.
Come, Lord,
be known among us.

O Key of David,
you open to us eternal life.
Come, Lord,
be known among us.

December 21

O Oriens

The Lord is my light and my salvation;
whom then shall I fear?
The Lord is my light and my salvation.
The Lord is the stronghold of my life;
of whom shall I be afraid?
The Lord is my light and my salvation.

Psalm 27:1

Christ is the Morning Star,
who, when the night of this world is past,
brings to his saints the promise of the light of life
and opens everlasting day.

Bede (c. 672–735)

O Morning Star, come;
bring light to all who are in darkness
and hope to those who face the shadow of death.

December 22

O Rex Gentium

Come to your world, O King of the Nations.
I look for you, I long for you.
I watch for you, I wait for you.

Come and rule in our hearts.
I look for you, I long for you.
I watch for you, I wait for you.

Come, be known to all people in all places.
I look for you, I long for you.
I watch for you, I wait for you.

Come, that the kingdoms of the world
may own your rule.
I look for you, I long for you.
I watch for you, I wait for you.

December 23

O Emmanuel

O Emmanuel, God with us,
open my eyes to your presence.
Maranatha.
Come, Lord Jesus.

Make my home your home.
Maranatha.
Come, Lord Jesus.

Make room in my life for you.
Maranatha.
Come, Lord Jesus.

O Emmanuel, God ever present,
reveal yourself to me.
Maranatha.
Come, Lord Jesus.

Christmas Eve

O God, who made this most hallowed night
resplendent with the glory of the true Light,
grant that we who have known
the mystery of that Light on earth,
may enter into the fullness of his joys in heaven.

Ancient Western Rite

Christmas Day

May we make room with the innkeeper
and know the joy of the shepherds,
the message of the angels,
the seeking of the wise men,
the bliss of Mary,
the presence of the Christ-child;
and may we rejoice
in the Word made flesh
dwelling among us.

December 26

O holy Child of Bethlehem,
descend to us, we pray;
cast out our sin, and enter in,
be born in us today.
We hear the Christmas angels
the great glad tidings tell:
O come to us, abide with us,
our Lord Emmanuel.

Phillips Brooks (1835–1893)

December 27

Though Christ a thousand times
in Bethlehem be born,
if he is not born in you,
you are still forlorn.

Angelus Silesius (1624–1677)

O come to my heart, Lord Jesus,
there is room in my heart for thee.

Emily Elizabeth Steele Elliott (1836–1897)

December 28

O God, I remember this day,
the slaughter of the holy innocents by King Herod.
I ask your blessing upon all suffering children,
upon all innocent victims,
and upon all who suffer from tyranny and violence.
I ask this in the name of him who suffered for me,
Christ my Lord.

December 29

Christ, for you there was no room at the inn;
you were taken as a refugee into Egypt,
a stranger in a foreign land.
I remember before you
all who are homeless,
all refugees and wandering people.
May I remember that in sharing with them
and caring for them
I reach out to you in each of them,
Christ my Lord.

December 30

Lord Jesus, Light of the World,
I pray for peace on earth
and goodwill among all peoples.
May I learn to accept your peace,
to share your peace,
to live your peace,
and to give your peace.
Lord Jesus, be known among us
and scatter the darkness from before us.

December 31

God, give us grace to accept with serenity
the things that cannot be changed,
courage to change the things that should be changed,
and the wisdom to know the difference.

Reinhold Niebuhr (1892–1971)

January 1

God bless my year with an awareness of you.

My dearest Lord,
be a bright flame before me,
a guiding star above me,
a smooth path beneath me,
and you a kindly shepherd behind me,
today and evermore.

St. Columba (521–597)

January 2

Lord our God,
grant me grace to desire you with my whole heart;
that so desiring you, I may seek and find you;
and so finding you, I may love you;
and so loving you, I may hate those sins
from which you have delivered me,
through Jesus Christ our Lord.

St. Anselm (1033–1109)

January 3

Eternal light, shine in our hearts;
Eternal goodness, deliver us from evil;
Eternal power, be our support;
Eternal wisdom, scatter the darkness of our ignorance;
Eternal pity, have mercy upon us;
that with all our heart and mind and strength
we may seek your face
and be brought by your infinite mercy
to your holy presence; through Jesus Christ our Lord.

Alcuin of York (735–804)

January 4

O my God, I give myself to you
in joy and in sorrow,
in sickness and in health,
in success and in failure,
in life and in death,
in time and for eternity.
Take me and keep me for your own;
through Jesus Christ my Lord.

Source unknown

January 5

Eternal God, the light of the minds that know you,
the joy of the hearts that love you,
the strength of the wills that serve you;
grant us so to know you that we may truly love you,
so to love you that we may freely serve you,
to the glory of your holy name.

St. Augustine of Hippo (354–430)

Epiphany

O God, who by the leading of a star
manifested your only Son to the peoples of the earth:
mercifully grant that we,
who know you now by faith,
may at last behold your glory face to face;
through Jesus Christ your Son our Lord,
who is alive and reigns with you,
in the unity of the Holy Spirit,
one God now and forever.

Collect for Epiphany, Common Worship

Lightning Source UK Ltd.
Milton Keynes UK
UKHW011837031220
374576UK00008B/189